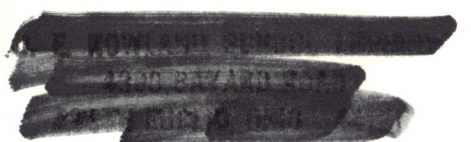

I want to be a TELEPHONE OPERATOR

by Eugene Baker

illustrated by Lois Axeman

CHILDRENS PRESS, CHICAGO

Library of Congress Cataloging in Publication Data

Baker, Eugene H.
  I Want to be a telephone operator.

  SUMMARY: Simple text and illustrations introduce the duties of a telephone operator.
  1. Telephone operators—Juvenile literature.
  [1. Telephone operators. 2. Occupations] I. Axeman, Lois, ill. II. Title. III. Title: Telephone operator.
HD8039.T3B34   384.6'4   74-28377
ISBN 0-516-01721-2

Copyright © 1975 by Regensteiner Publishing Enterprises, Inc.
All rights reserved. Published simultaneously in Canada.
Printed in the United States of America.

1 2 3 4 5 6 7 8 9 10 11 12 R 78 77 76 75

"I got the job!" Gene called. He rushed into the house.

Dan, Gene's brother, was eating. "Great," he smiled, "what is it?" Gene was out of high school. Dan knew he had been looking for a job.

"I'm going to work for the telephone company," Gene said. "I start Monday. I will train to be a telephone operator. The starting pay is good. Later I may go into sales."

"How come they picked you?" Dan asked.

"I'm not sure," Gene answered. "A lot of people must have seen the Help Wanted ad in the newspaper. The personnel office at the telephone company was crowded. When my turn came, they gave

me a form that asked many questions. Then I talked to a man about work. He asked if I was good in math and English in school. Then he asked me to take a test. It took two hours."

"Wow," moaned Dan, "just like school."

Gene laughed. "You're right, but I must have done well. They said I could work in many different jobs. Some inside . . . some outside. The personnel man explained each job. He sure was nice to me."

"Can I see you at work some time?" asked Dan.

"Let's wait and see," said Gene. "I have to go through a training program first."

Gene started his job training. He learned many things. He learned how to use the switchboard. He learned how to record the time of a long distance call and the cost. He also learned what to do in emergencies.

After a few weeks he received permission for Dan to visit. That night, Gene said, "Dan, do you want to see where I work? Tomorrow is Saturday. If we go early, I can show you around."

"I sure would," smiled Dan.

The boys were up and out early. When they arrived at the telephone company, Gene warned, "Dan, please don't touch anything. But it's okay to ask questions."

"I'm good at that," laughed Dan.

Inside the front door was a large display of telephone equipment. "Look at how the telephone has changed," said Dan. "There is no dial. Look at the funny crank."

Gene showed Dan the locker room. They hung up their coats. Down the hall they looked in the lunchroom. "This is where I eat," said Gene.

"Over in this room is where we keep our telephone headsets. Each operator has his own. Want to try mine on?"

"It feels funny," Dan said, "but it doesn't weigh much. I look like an astronaut."

"Come on," said Gene, "I want you to meet my supervisor." They carefully put the headset away. Then they walked to a large room. Many telephone operators were working. One woman, standing behind the operators, came over.

"Hello, Donna," said Gene. "I would like you to meet my brother, Dan. Dan, Donna is my supervisor."

"Happy to meet you," smiled Donna. "Your brother is learning to be a fine telephone operator. It's time for my break. Do you want me to show you around?"

"Yes I would," answered Dan.

They entered a room where several people were sitting in front of large panels. These panels had many buttons and switches and plugs. "These are called switchboards," said Donna.

"This switchboard is for long distance calls. Calls that are outside of our local area. These operators are called toll operators. They help people make long distance calls. They can call anywhere in the world. New York, London, Australia, or South America.

They keep a record of the time and cost. This cost is then charged to the customer. Operators use geography every day in handling long distance calls."

"I work here," said Gene. "It's interesting."

On the next floor they stopped in another room. "Here we have another kind of operator. We call them D.A.'s for directory assistance operators."

"Look at all of the phone books!" exclaimed Dan. "How do they find anything?"

"The books are arranged by area," Donna replied. "They are alphabetical. The operators can find a phone number in just a few moments. D.A.'s are very good at spelling and using numbers."

After watching for a few moments, they stopped in front of a huge display. "Here are some of the other jobs at our company," said Donna.

Dan looked carefully at several pictures. "Hey, that's a girl climbing that pole!"

"Yes," smiled Donna. "She's in telephone repair."

"Well," said Dan, "I sure learned a lot. Thank you for the tour."

"Oh, you're welcome," said Donna. "Here are a few booklets that explain more about the telephone company. This one tells how Alexander Graham Bell invented the telephone."

Dan looked up at Gene. "I think I may be a telephone operator when I go to work."

"Really?" said Gene. "How come?"

"Well," answered Dan, "if I'm an operator, I can tell everyone that my name is on every telephone in the world."

Everyone laughed.

ABOUT THE AUTHOR:

Dr. Baker was graduated from Carthage College, Carthage, Illinois. He got his master's degree and doctorate in education at Northwestern University. He has worked as a teacher, as a principal, and as a director of curriculum and instruction. Now he works full time as a curriculum consultant. His practical help to schools where new programs are evolving is sparked with his boundless enthusiasm. He likes to see social studies and language arts taught with countless resources and many books to encourage students to think independently, creatively, and critically. The Bakers, who live in Arlington Heights, Illinois, have a son and two daughters.

ABOUT THE ARTIST

Lois Axeman is a native Chicagoan who lives with her husband and two children in the city. After attending the American Academy and the Institute of Design (IIT), Lois started as a fashion illustrator in a department store. When the children's wear illustrator became ill, Lois took her place and found she loved drawing children. She started free-lancing then, and has been doing text and picture books ever since.